LEARN TO
READ AND WRITE

Alphabet Workbook

Volume 1 • 2016

ISBN: 9780989421300

Find the letters in your name and color them in.

a	b	c	d	e	f
g	h	i	j	k	l
m	n	o	p	q	r
s	t	u	v	w	x
y	z				

Place your name label here ⬇.

Alphabet Workbook

© Heritage Text

Read the abc chart with your class.

a	b	c	d	e	f	f
g	h	i	j	k	l	l
m	n	o	p	q	r	s	s
t	u	v	w	x	y	z	z
a	e	i	o	u		

Alphabet Workbook

RIGHT & LEFT

Circle all animals in the **right** column facing **right** and all animals in the **left** column facing **left**. Then color them.

 left   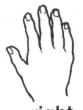 right

1.

2.

3.

4.

5.

Alphabet Workbook   © Heritage Text

Trace the lines to help each animal find its home.

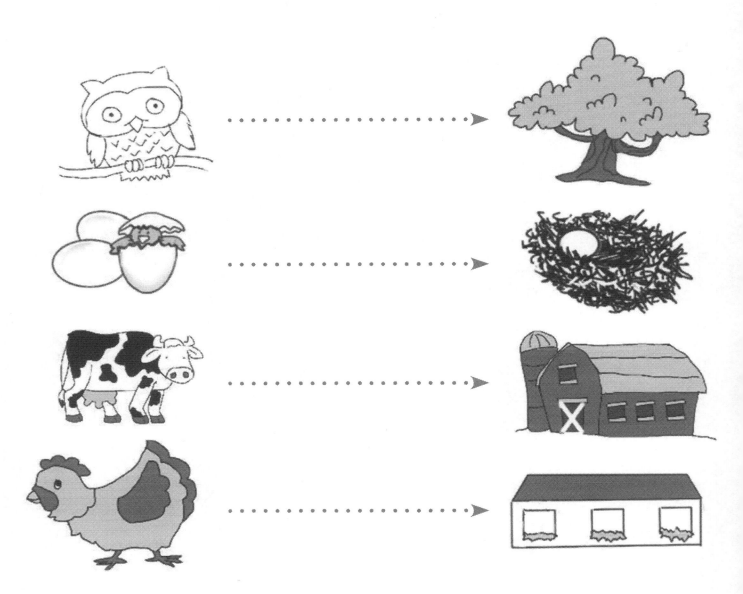

Trace the dotted lines from left to right.

Alphabet Workbook

 Trace the dotted lines from left to right.

 Trace the lines to help the animal find its home.

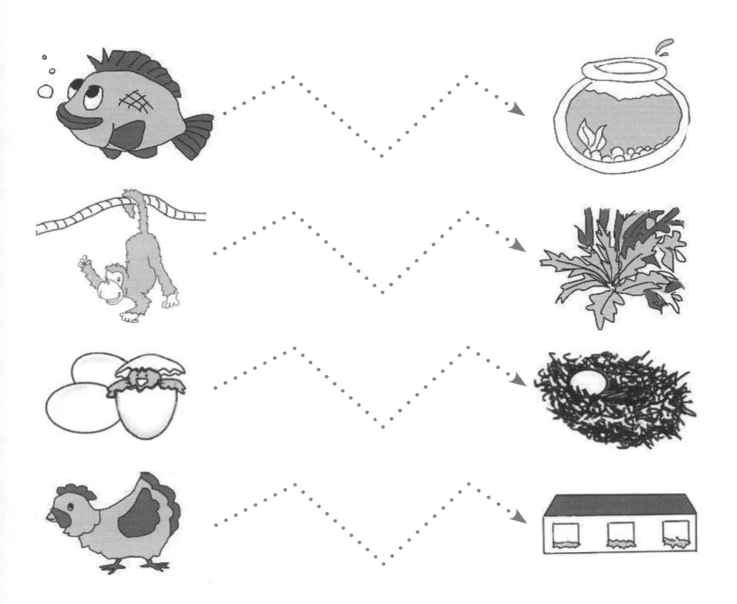

Alphabet Workbook

Trace the dotted lines from top to bottom.

Trace the dotted lines from top to bottom.

Alphabet Workbook

 Trace the dotted lines from left to right.

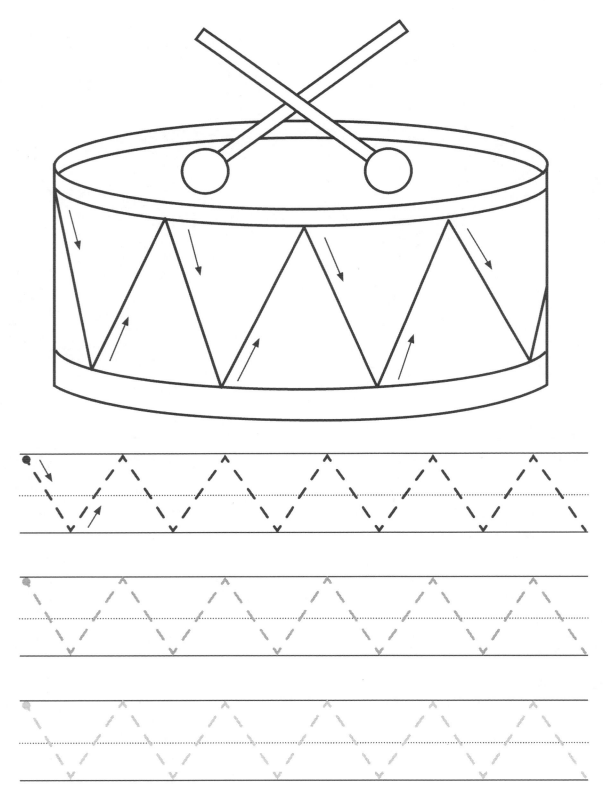

Trace the lines to help the animal find its home.

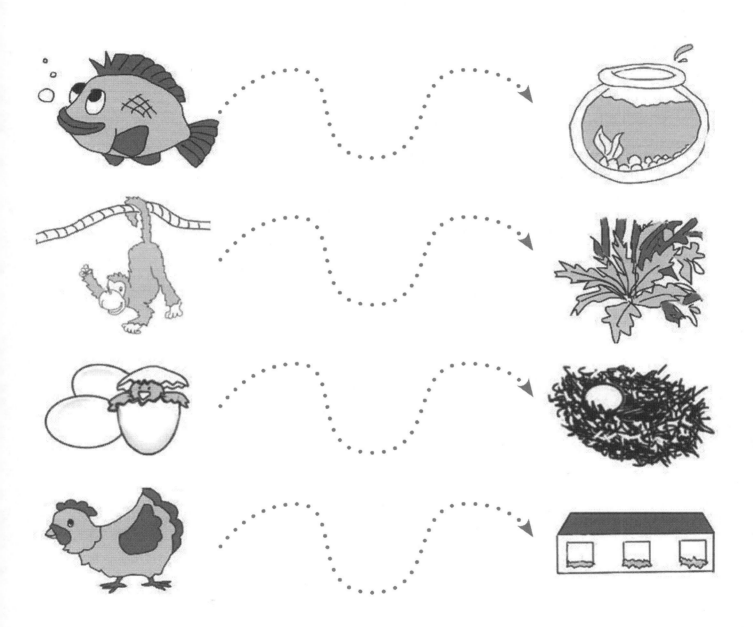

Alphabet Workbook

© Heritage Text

 Trace the dotted circles starting at the top.

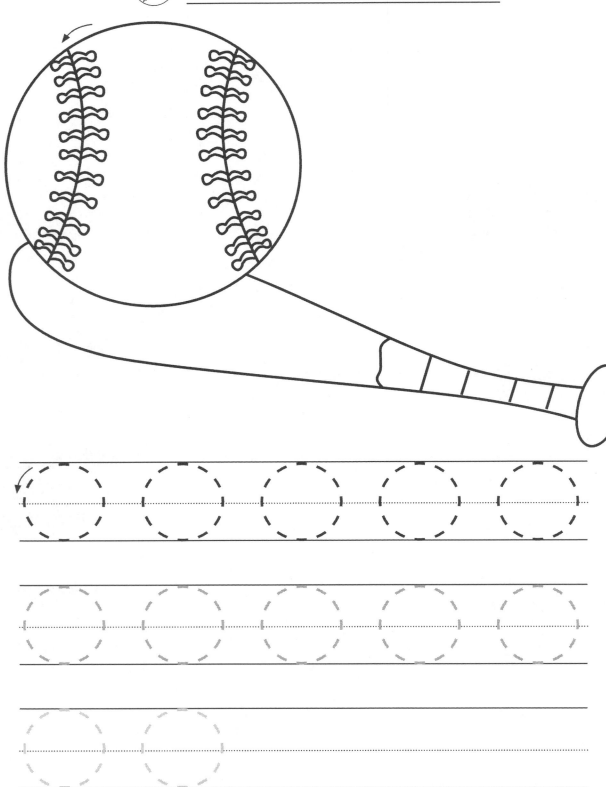

© Heritage Text

Alphabet Workbook

Trace the dotted half-circles starting from the top left.

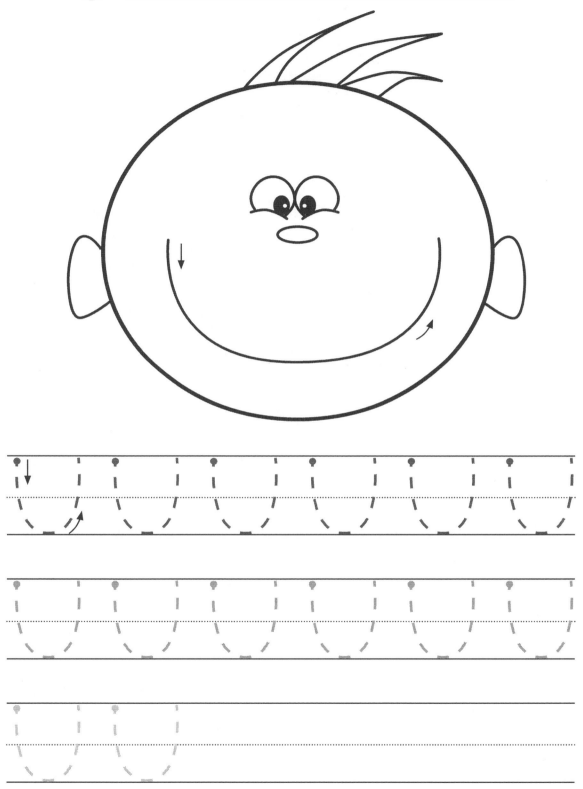

Alphabet Workbook

Trace the dotted half-circles starting from the bottom left.

Alphabet Workbook

Read the abc chart with your class.

a	b	c	d	e	f	f
g	h	i	j	k	l	l
m	n	o	p	q	r	s	s
t	u	v	w	x	y	z	z
a	e	i	o	u		

Alphabet Workbook

© Heritage Text

Connect the **dots** to form a picture.

a

c   d

b

e

a b c d e

Alphabet Workbook

Draw pictures of words that begin with letter *a*

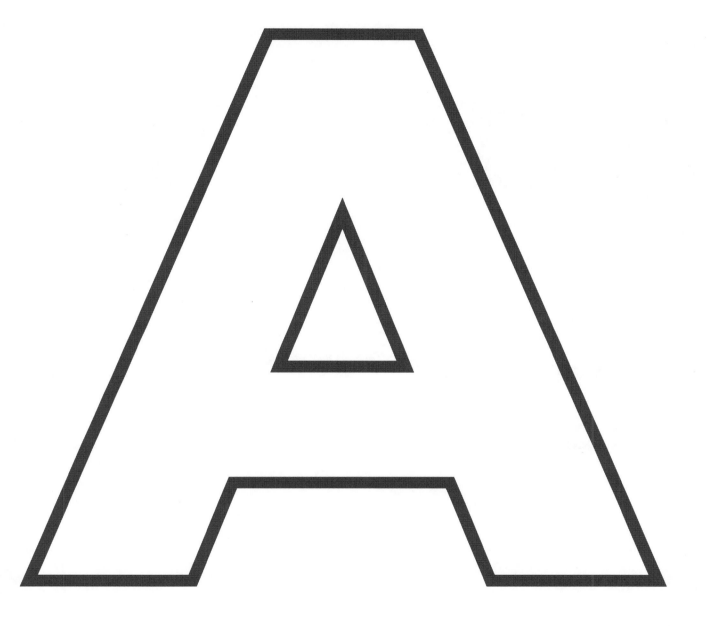

✏️ Write the letter **a**.

Alphabet Workbook

Write the letter **a**.

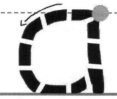

Alphabet Workbook

© Heritage Text

Write the letter **a**.

© Heritage Text

Alphabet Workbook

 Trace the letters **Aa**. Say the word that names each picture. Color each picture whose name begins with the same sound as **apple**, and draw a line from these pictures to the letters **Aa**.

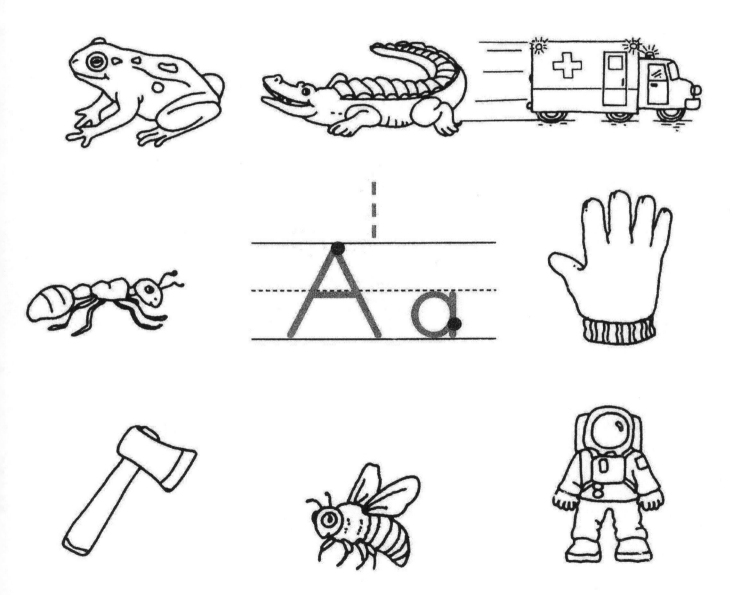

Alphabet Workbook

© Heritage Text

 Write the letter **a**. Say the word that names each picture. Listen for the sound in the **middle** of the word. Color each picture whose name has the same middle sound as **cat**.

__a__

Name _____

_____

Alphabet Workbook

 Listen for short *a*. Name each picture. If it has the short *a* sound, draw a line to the

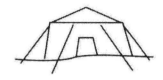

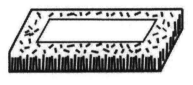

mat

Alphabet Workbook

 Circle the pictures that have the short **a** sound in the **middle** of the word.

Alphabet Workbook

Aa | _a_

Name _____

Say the name of the picture. Where do you hear the sound /a/a? Draw a circle around the first *a* if it is the beginning sound (as in *apple*). Draw a circle around the second *a* if it is the middle sound (as in *cat*).

Alphabet Workbook

 Cut out the pictures and sort them on the following page.

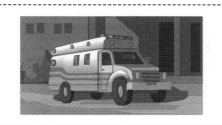

Alphabet Workbook

Paste the pictures whose words begin with the short *a* sound in the first column and words that have the short *a* sound in the middle in the second column

a

and

a

a

a

Alphabet Workbook

Say the picture names and word in each row. Underline the word **and**.

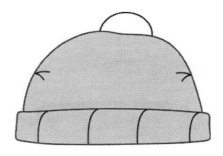

and

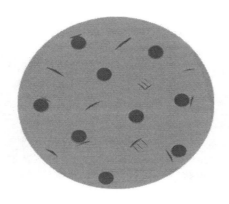

and

and

Color all the rams facing the *left*.

left

Alphabet Workbook

© Heritage Text

Color all the cats facing the **right**.

right

Alphabet Workbook

Look at the pictures at the top of the page. One bird is facing **left**. One bird is facing **right**. then, look at the rest of the pictures. Circle the pictures that show animals facing **right**. Draw a line under the pictures that show animals facing **left**.

Alphabet Workbook

© Heritage Text

Help the cat find her *kittens*.

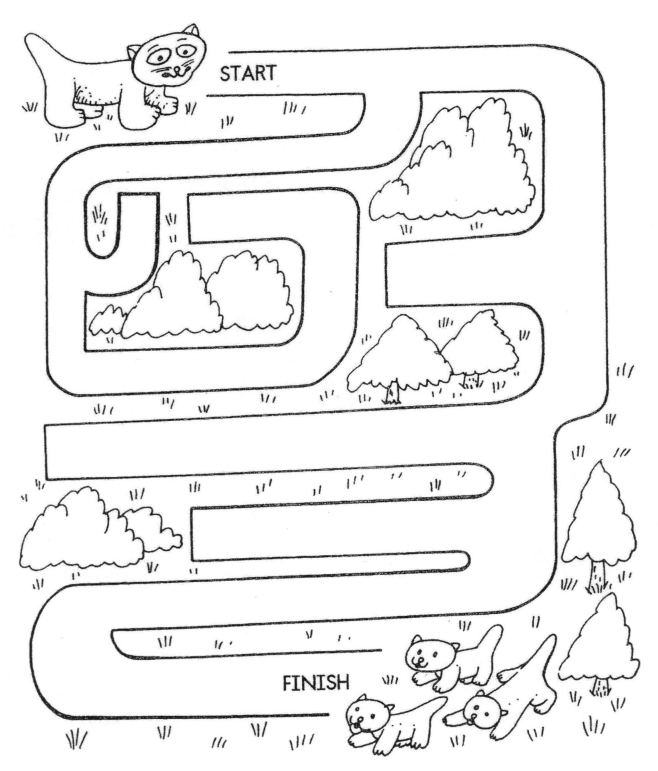

START

FINISH

Alphabet Workbook

Help the children find their way to *school*.

START

SCHOOL

FINISH

Alphabet Workbook

 Draw a line from let to right to connect the person with the place where he or she is going.

Alphabet Workbook

 Practice the letter **A**.

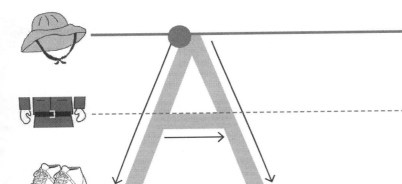

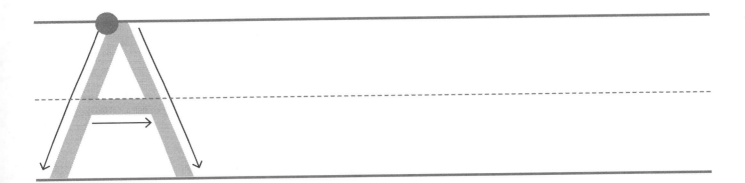

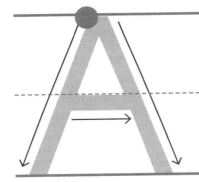

Alphabet Workbook

© Heritage Text

Color the capital **A** red. Then color the ant.

Alphabet Workbook

Draw pictures of words that begin with letter **n**

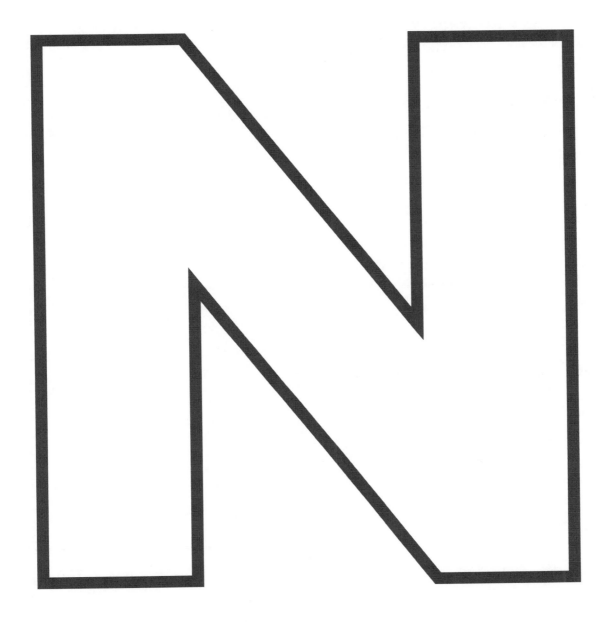

Nn

 Write the letter **n**.

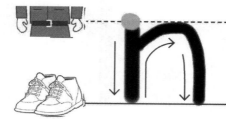 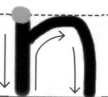 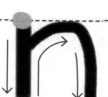

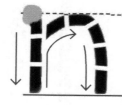

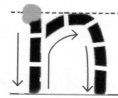

Alphabet Workbook

 Write the letter **n**, **a**.

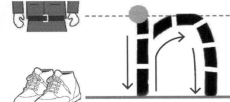

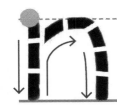

Alphabet Workbook

© Heritage Text

Nn

 Write the letters **n**, **a**, **an**, and **na**.

© Heritage Text

Alphabet Workbook

 Trace the letters **Nn**. Say the word that names each picture.
Color each picture whos name begins with the same sound as
nest, and draw a line from these pictures to the letters **Nn**.

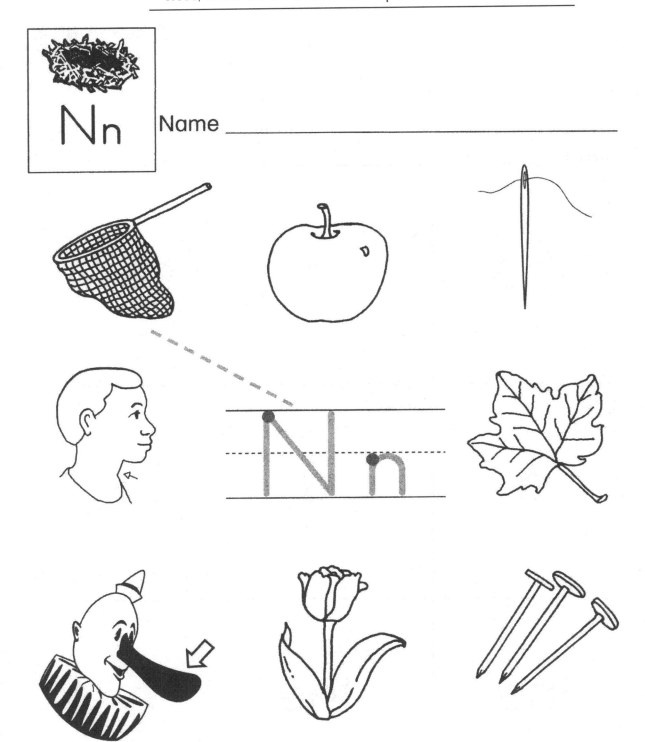

Name _____

Alphabet Workbook

Nn

 Say the name of each picture. Write the letter **n** under each picture that has the same ending sound as **fan**.

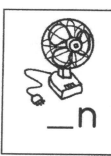

_n | Name _____

(lion)	(balloon)	(cap)
n		
(duck)	(hen)	10

Alphabet Workbook

Say the name of each picture. Where do you hear the sound /n/**n**? Draw a circle around the first **n** to show if it is the beginning sound (as in **nest**). Draw a circle around the second **n** to show if it is the ending sound (as in **fan**).

Nn	_n

Name _____

n　　(n)	n　　　n
n　　　n	n　　　n
n　　　n	n　　　n

© Heritage Text

 Say the name of each picture. Draw a circle around the letter that stands for the sound you hear at the **beginning** of each picture name.

Nn | **Aa**   Name _____

(apple)
n
a

(star)
n
a

(tree)
n
a

(fish)
n
a

(flower)
n
a

(butterfly)
n
a

Alphabet Workbook

 Write the letter **n**. Draw a line from the letter **n** to each picture whose name ends with the same sound as **fan**.

☆ Write the letter **a**. Draw a line to each picture whose name has the same middle sound as **cat**.

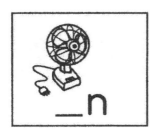

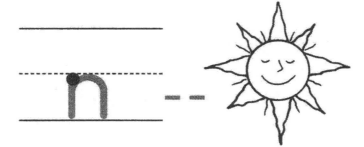

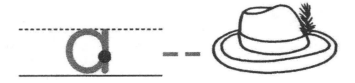

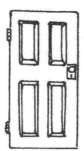

Alphabet Workbook

© Heritage Text

Look at the first picture. ☆ Draw a circle around the picture whose name has the same *beginning* sound. ⌂ Draw a circle around the picture whose name has the same *ending* sound. ↩ Draw a circle around the picture whos name has the same *middle* sound.

 **Nn**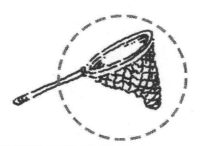

 **Aa**

 **__n**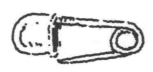

 **__a__**

Alphabet Workbook

Cut out the pictures and sort them on the following page.

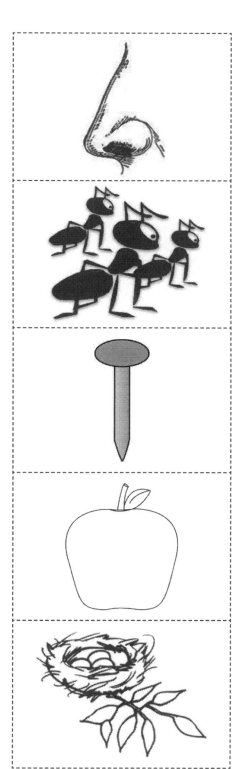

ABCDEF
GHIJKLM
NOPQRS
TUVWXYZ

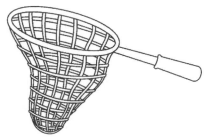

Aa   Nn

a n

a n

a n

a n

Alphabet Workbook

 Blend the letters to read the words.
Then, draw a picture of Ann and Nan in the box.

Ann =

Ann

Nan =

Nan

Alphabet Workbook

 Read the phrases. Match the phrases to the pictures.

Nan and Ann

Nan

Ann

Alphabet Workbook

 my

---

 the

Alphabet Workbook

Nn

 ○ ☆ Say the word and picture name. Draw a circle around the word **my**. 🌲 Draw a picture of something you play with after the word **my**. Then draw a circle around the word **my**.

my

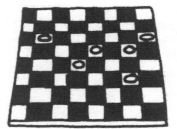

my

my

Alphabet Workbook

Say the word and picture name. Draw a circle around the word in *front* of the picture.

a

the

my

the

Alphabet Workbook

© Heritage Text

 Read each word and say the picture name. Draw a circle around the word **and**. Draw a line under the word **my**. Draw two lines under the word **a**. Draw a picture of two things that belong to you.

my  and

a  and

my and

Alphabet Workbook

Draw a line to match the *opposites*.

boy

night

happy

girl

day

closed

open

sad

Alphabet Workbook

 Draw a line to match the **opposites**.

small

moon

open

girl

boy

big

sun

closed

Alphabet Workbook

 Draw a line to match the **opposites**.

empty

small

big

full of air

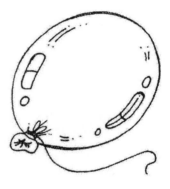

flat

full

Alphabet Workbook

© Heritage Text

Practice the letter **N**.

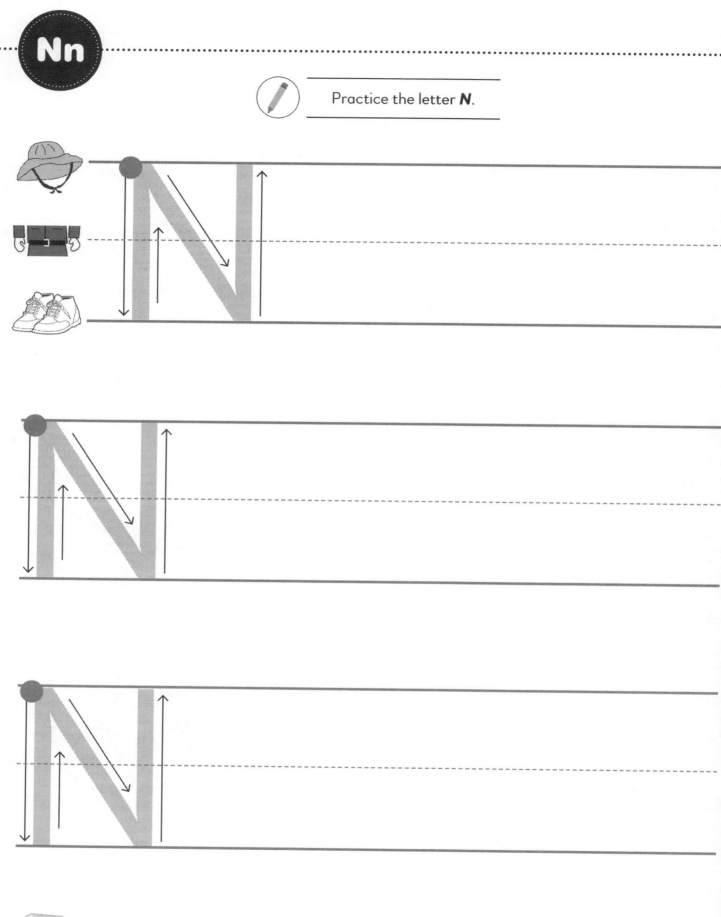

Alphabet Workbook

 Practice the letter **N**.

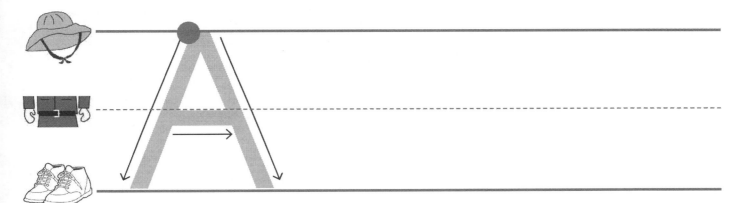

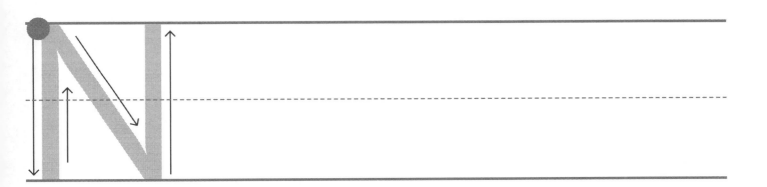

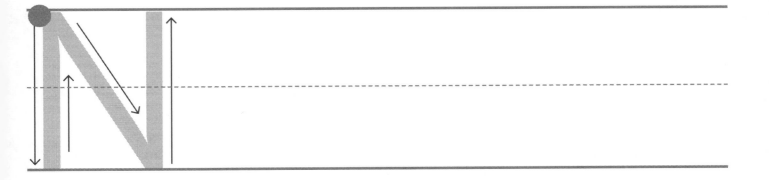

Alphabet Workbook

© Heritage Text

 Color the capital **N**s purple and the lowercase **n**s grey to find the hidden picture.

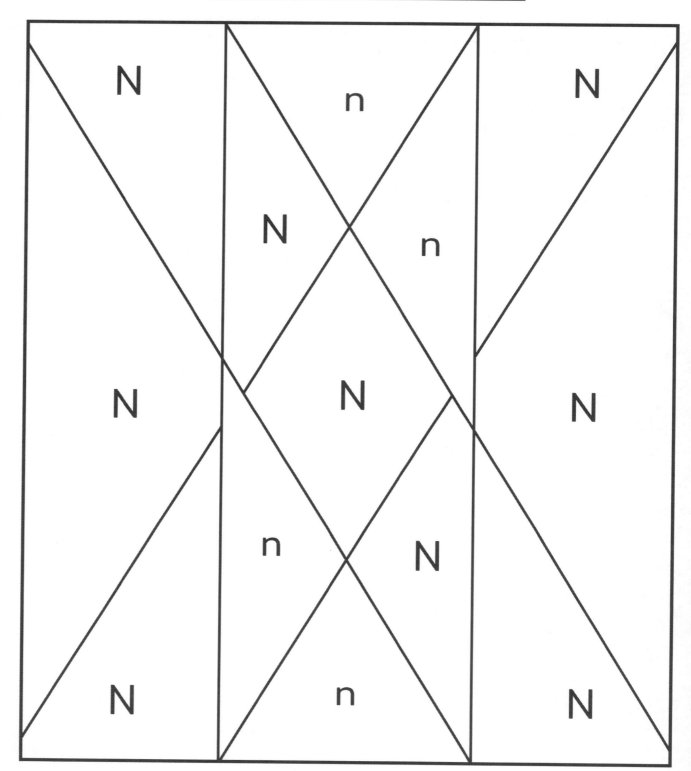

© Heritage Text

Alphabet Workbook

Draw pictures of words that begin with letter **r**

 Write the letter **r**.

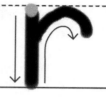 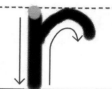

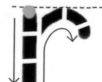

Alphabet Workbook

 Write the letters *r*, *a* and *n*.

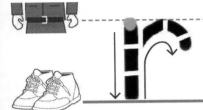

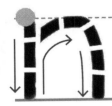

Alphabet Workbook

© Heritage Text

 Write the letters **r**, **ar**, **ra** and **ran**.

r

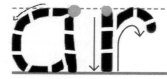

ar

ra

ran

Alphabet Workbook

Name each picture. If the picture begins with the sound **r**, draw a line to the ***rocket***.

rocket

Alphabet Workbook

Rr

 Write the letter **r**. Say the word that names each picture. Color the picture whose name begins with the same sound as **rope**.

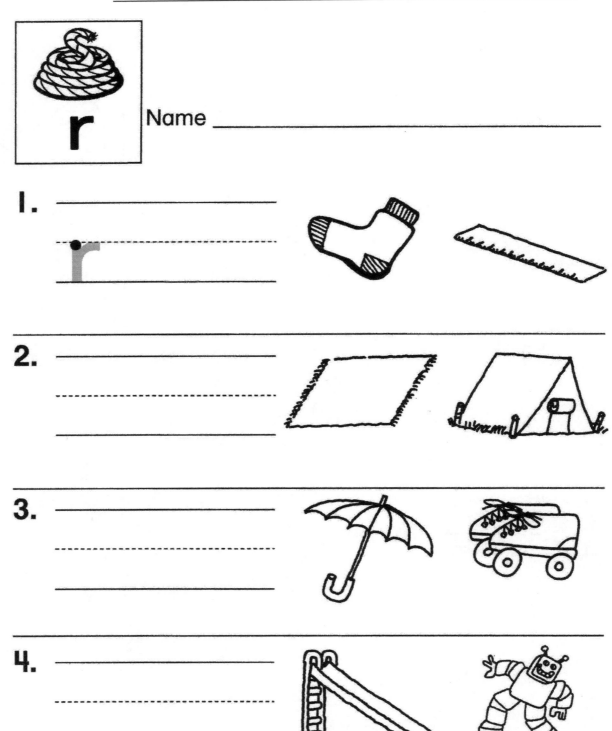

r

Name _____

1. _____

    r ------------------------

    _____

2. _____

    _____

3. _____

    _____

4. _____

    _____

Alphabet Workbook

Look what I can read!!

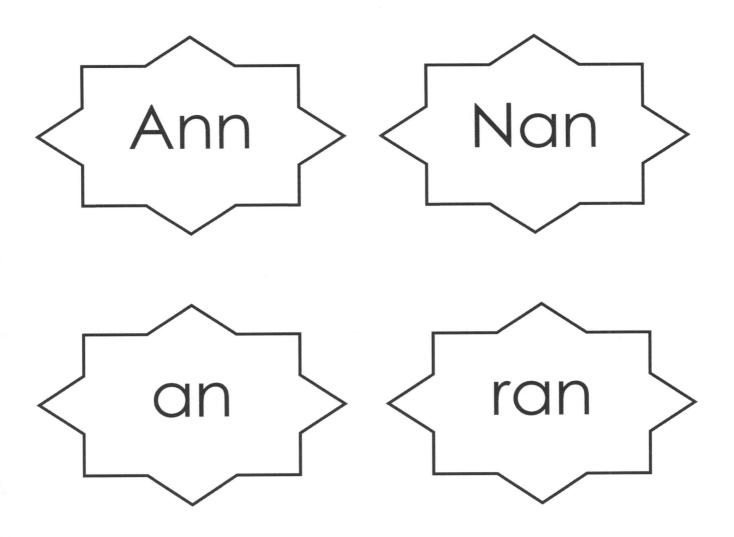

Ann

Nan

an

ran

 Read the sentences. Then, use the words below to complete the sentences.

_____

\- - - - - - - - - - - - - - - - - -

_____

_____

\- - - - - - - - - - - - - - - - - -

_____

_____

\- - - - - - - - - - - - - - - - - -

_____

| Ann | Nan | ran |

Alphabet Workbook

 Read the sentences. Then, use the words below to complete the sentences.

Nan ran.

Ann ran.

Nan ran _____ .

Ann ran _____ .

Use of prepositions;

(to the, around the...)

Alphabet Workbook

 Read the sentences. Then, use the words below to complete the sentences.

Nan and Ann ran.

Nan and Ann ran _____ .

Nan and Ann ran _____ .

Choose from these prepositions:

to the
around the

Alphabet Workbook

 I

 that

Alphabet Workbook

  Read the sentences by saying the word and telling the picture. Draw a circle around the word **I**. Draw a picture of yourself doing something to help out after the word **I**. Then draw a circle around the word **I**.

I

I

I

I

 ☆○ Say the word and picture name. Draw a circle around the word ***that***. 🌲 Draw a picture of an animal after the word ***that***. Then draw a circle around the word ***that***.

○

that

☆

that

🌲

that

Alphabet Workbook

Rr

 Look at the *pattern* in each row. Circle the pictures that continue each *pattern*. Then, color the pictures.

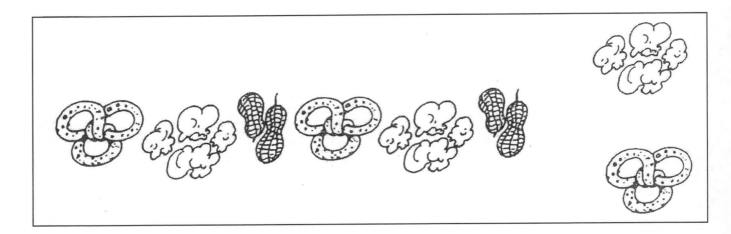

Alphabet Workbook

 Look at the *pattern* in each row. Draw the pictures that continue each *pattern*. Then, color the pictures.

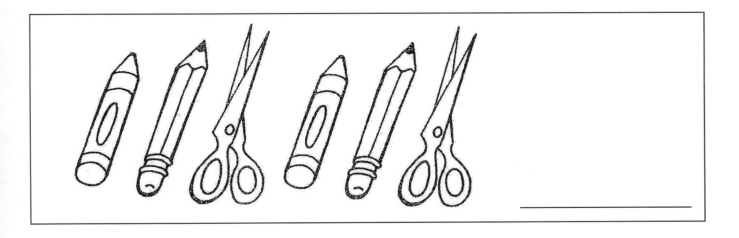

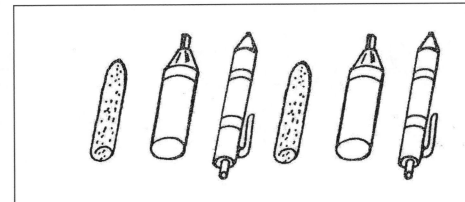

Alphabet Workbook

Look at the pictures. Write a **1** in the box that showed what happened *first*.
Write a **2** in the box that showed what happened *second*.
Write a **3** in the box that showed what happened *third*.
Then, color the pictures.

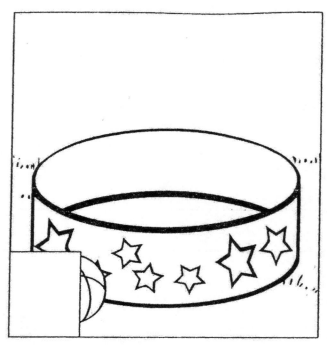

Alphabet Workbook

Look at the pictures. Write a **1** in the box that showed what happened *first*.
Write a **2** in the box that showed what happened *second*.
Write a **3** in the box that showed what happened *third*.
Then, color the pictures.

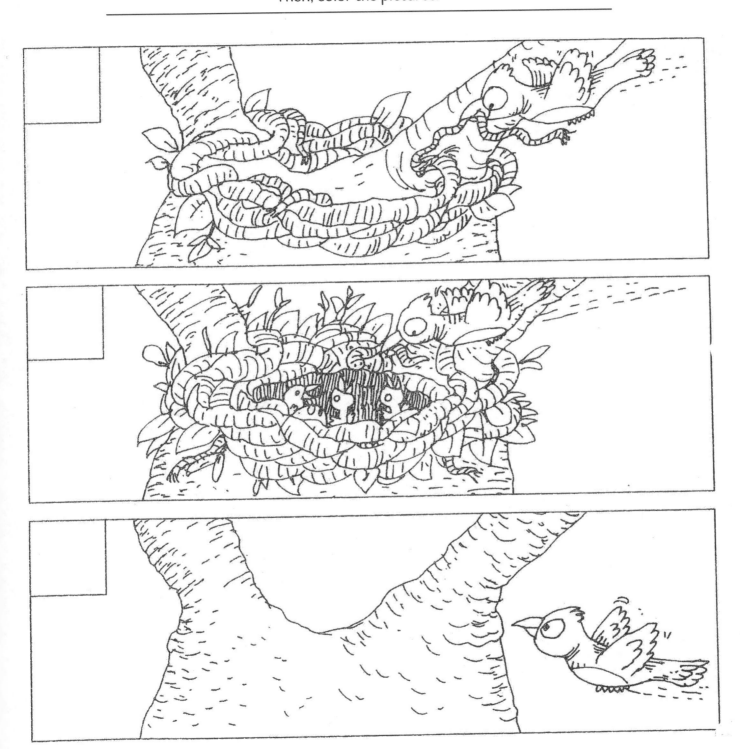

Alphabet Workbook

Rr

Practice the letter **R**.

Alphabet Workbook

Practice the letter **R**.

Alphabet Workbook

 Color the capital **R**s yellow. Then color the lowercase **r**s red to reveal a hidden picture.

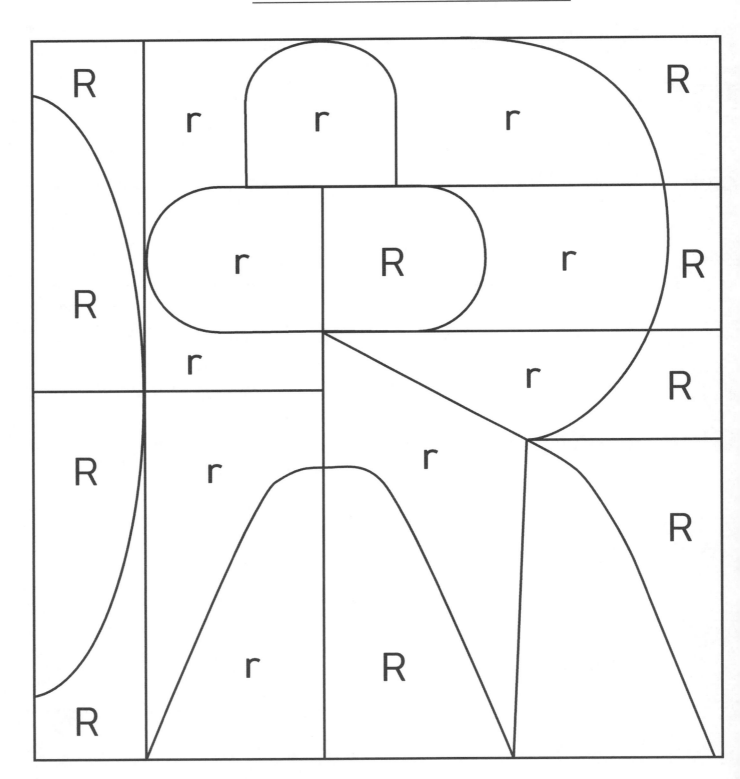

© Heritage Text

Alphabet Workboo

Draw pictures of words that begin with letter **d**

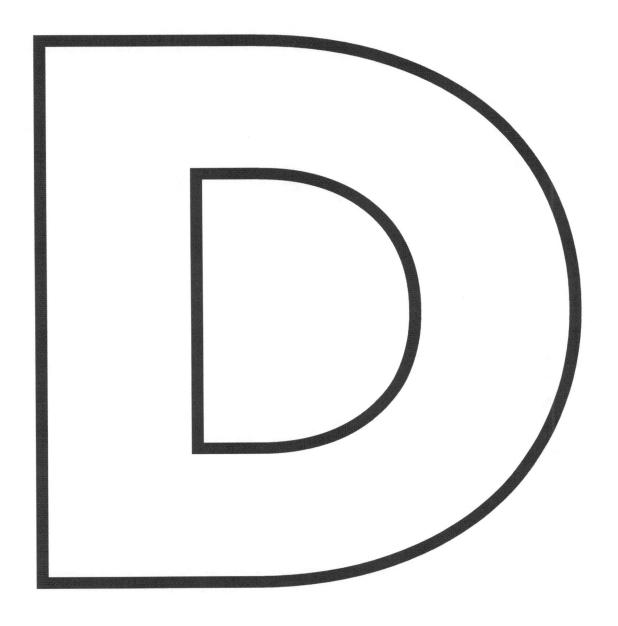

Dd

 Write the letter **d**.

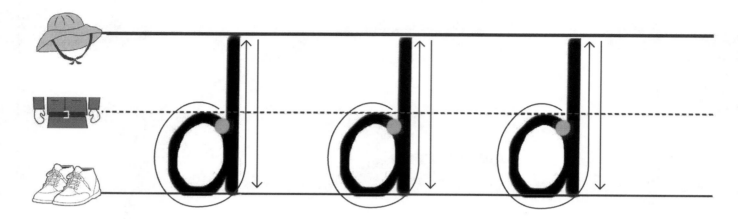

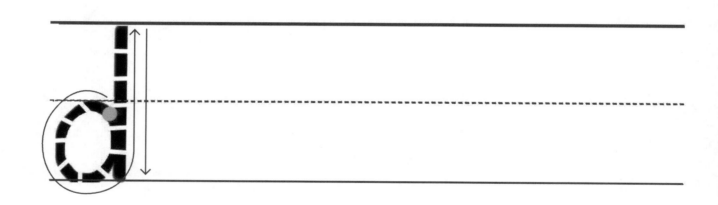

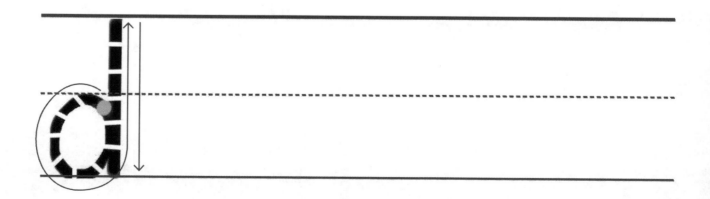

Alphabet Workbook

 Write the letters **d**, **r** and **n**.

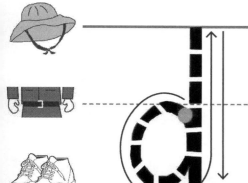

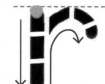

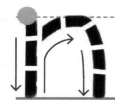

Alphabet Workbook

© Heritage Text

Dd

Write the letters **d**, **ad**, **dr**, and **and**.

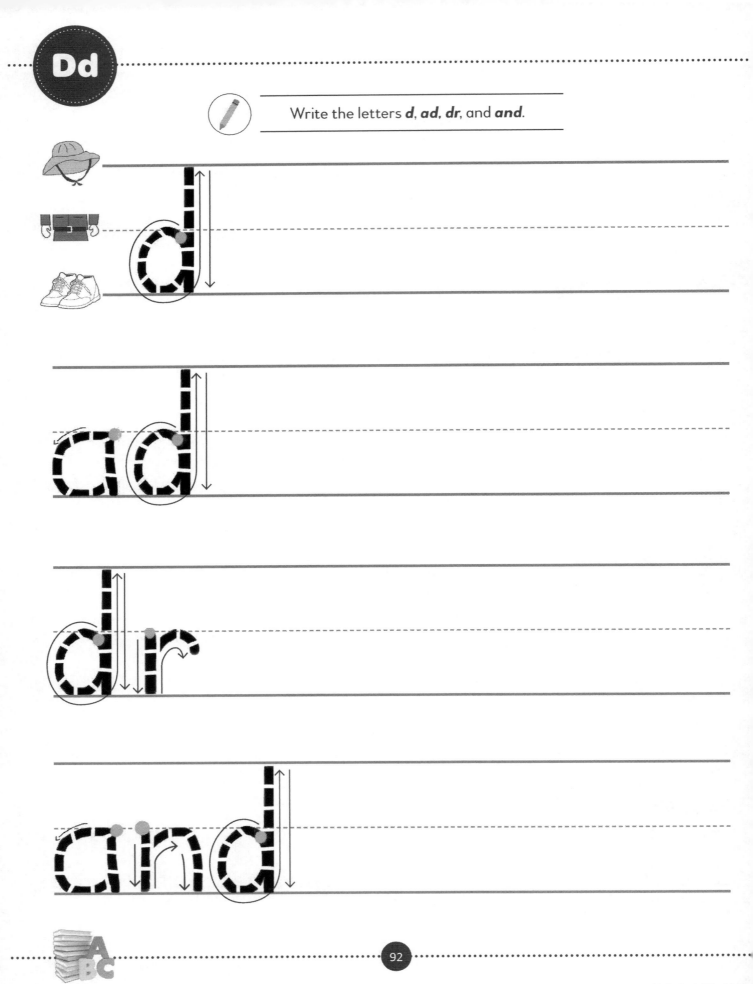

Alphabet Workboo

 Trace the letters **Dd**. Say the word that names each picture. Color each picture who's name begins with the same sound as **duck**. Draw a line from these pictures to the letters **Dd**.

 Name _____

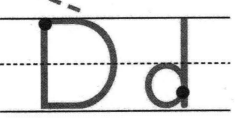

Alphabet Workbook

Dd

 Say the name of the pictures in each row. Color the picture whos name has the same ending sound as **bed**. Write the letter **d**.

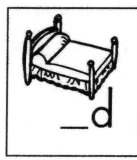

Name _____

  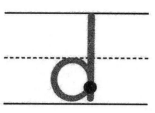

 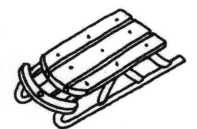

Alphabet Workbook

Say the name of the picture. Where do you hear the sound /d/**d**?
Draw a circle around the first **d** if it is the beginning sound (as in **duck**).
Draw a circle around the second **d** if it is the ending sond (as in **bed**).

Name _____

Alphabet Workbook

© Heritage Text

Listen for Dd

Name each picture. If it begins with the **/d/** sound, draw a line to the 🐕. If it ends with the **/d/** sound, draw a line to the 😞.

dog   **sad**

Alphabet Workbook

Cut out the pictures and sort them on the following page.

Alphabet Workbook

© Heritage Text

Alphabet Workbook

Dd   Rr

Alphabet Workbook

Dd

 Read the word, tap out the sounds of the word. Then, circle the number of sounds and write the word on the line.

an	1 2 3 4 5	_____
Nan	1 2 3 4 5	_____
ran	1 2 3 4 5	_____
Dan	1 2 3 4 5	_____

Alphabet Workbook

 Read the word. Write it on the line.
Draw a line to the correct picture.

d a d

D a n

_____

_____

_ _ _ _ _ _ _ _ _ _ _ _ _

_ _ _ _ _ _ _ _ _ _ _ _ _

_____

_____

Iphabet Workbook

© Heritage Text

Dd

 Look at the picture. Read the names. Draw a line under the name that goes with the picture. Write the name.

<u>Dan</u> Nan

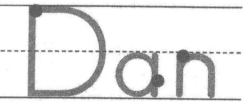

Dan Nan

_____

- - - - - - - - - - - - - - -

_____

Dan Nan

_____

- - - - - - - - - - - - - - -

_____

Dan Nan

_____

- - - - - - - - - - - - - - -

_____

Dan Nan

_____

- - - - - - - - - - - - - - -

_____

Alphabet Workbook

Practice Reading

1. an
2. ran
3. Nan
4. Ann
5. add

6. dad
7. Dan
8. ad

1. <u>My</u> dad.

2. <u>My</u> dad ran.

3. Dan ran.

4. <u>My</u> dad <u>and</u> Nan ran.

5. Dan ran.

6. <u>My</u> dad, Nan <u>and</u> Dan ran.

7. <u>I</u> ran.

8. <u>My</u> dad, Nan, Dan, <u>and</u> <u>I</u> ran.

Iphabet Workbook

  Say each word and picture name. Draw a circle around the word **and**.
Draw a circle around the word **I**. Next to the word **my** draw a picture of something or someone you love. Then draw a circle around the word **my**.

 and

my  and

I  my  .

Alphabet Workboo

Say the word at the beginning of each row. Draw a circle around the word where you see it in the same row.

a	the	(a)
my	my	that
the	that	the
that	that	my

Iphabet Workbook

 Say the word and picture name. Draw a circle around the word in front of the picture.

the

a

that

my

Alphabet Workbook

Read the first word in each row. Find the same word in the row and underline it.

an	in	on	<u>an</u>
and	and	hand	land
I	in	it	I
my	mi	muy	my
the	the	tet	ten
a	an	a	at
that	hat	that	thin

Dd

 Color and cut out the pictures at the bottom of the page. Glue them in the correct place.

under	on
between	**in**

 Look at the picture. The sun is above the bird.
Draw an **X** on the pictures **below** the bird.

Iphabet Workbook

Practice the letter **D**.

Alphabet Workbo

Practice the words.

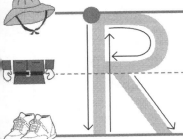 R

Dan

Dad

Nan

Alphabet Workbook

 Color the capital **D**s blue. Then color the lowercase **d**s red to reveal a hidden picture.

D   D   d

                                d

D   d   D

              d

D   d

          d   D

D   D

          D   d
                          d

© Heritage Text

Alphabet Workbook

Draw pictures of words that begin with letter *m*

Mm

Write the letter **m**.

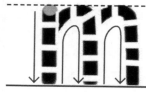

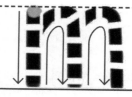

Alphabet Workbook

 Write the letter **m**, **n**, and **d**.

Alphabet Workbook

Mm

Write the letter *am*, *ma*, *man*, and *mad*.

Alphabet Workbook

Trace the letters **Mm**. Say the word that names each picture. Color each picture whos name begins with the same sound as *moon*, and draw a line from these pictures to the letters **Mm**.

Name _____

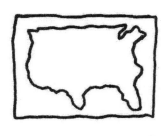

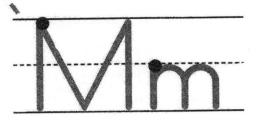

lphabet Workbook

© Heritage Text

Mm

 Say the name of each picture. Color the picture whos name has the same ending sound as **drum**. Write the letter **m**.

_m   Name _____

_____

m

_____

_____

Alphabet Workbook

Say the name of the picture. Where do you hear the sound /m/**m**?
Draw a circle around the first **m** if it is the beginning sound (as in **moon**).
Draw a circle around the second **m** if it is the ending sound (as in **drum**).

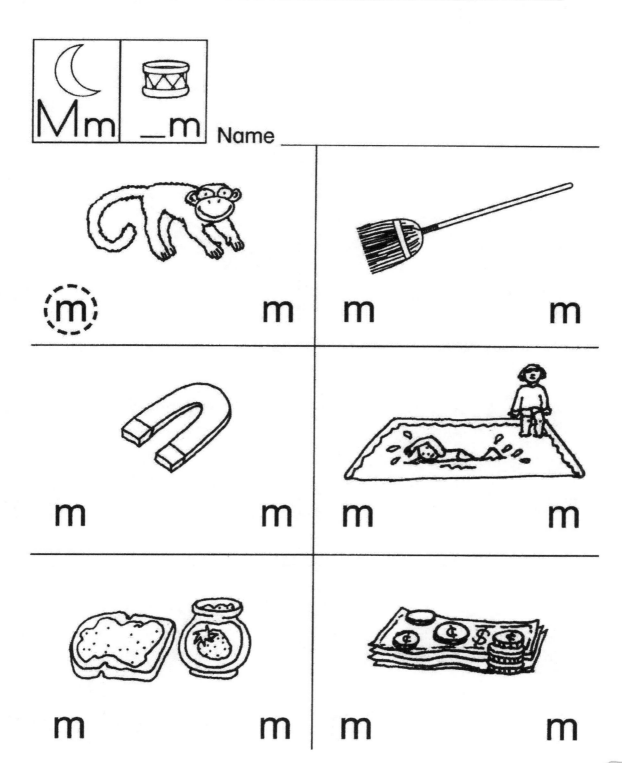

| M m | _m | Name _____ |

m   m   m

m   m   m   m

m   m   m   m

lphabet Workbook

 Say the name of each picture. Draw a circle around the letter that stands for the sound you hear at the end of each picture name.

_d   _m

Name _____

Alphabet Workboc

 Cut out the pictures and sort them on the following page.

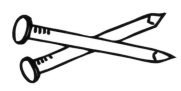

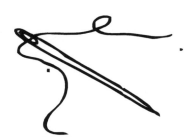

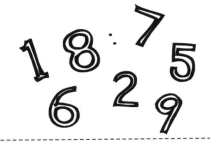

Alphabet Workbook

© Heritage Text

122

Alphabet Workboo

Nn Mm

Listen for Mm

Help the 🧍 get to the 🏡 . Say the name of each picture. If it begins with the sound for **m**, 🖍 it blue. If it ends with the sound for **m**, 🖍 it yellow.

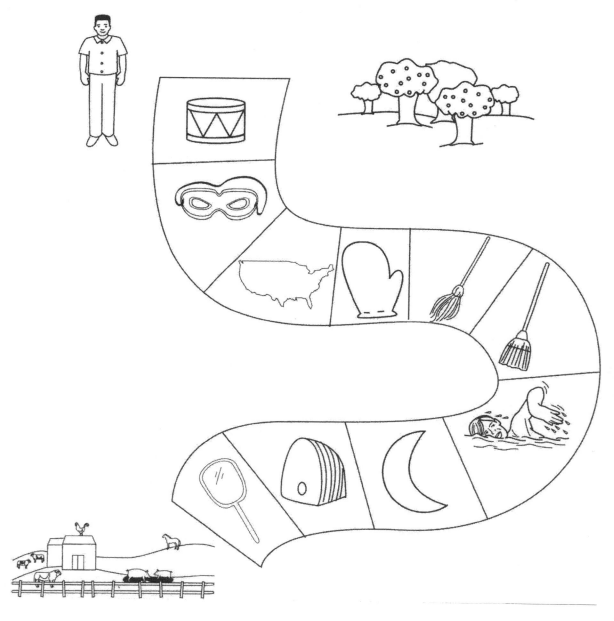

Alphabet Workbook

is

big

Alphabet Workbook

© Heritage Text

 🍎 Use your red crayon. Color the two items in the sentence. Read the sentence: **A heart is red.**

☆ Use your yellow crayon. Color the two items in the sentence. Read the sentence: **A banana is yellow.**

🌲 Use your green crayon. Color the two items in the sentence. Read the sentence: **A leaf is green.**

Then draw a line under the word *is* in each sentence.

🍎 A ♡ is ⬡ .

☆ A 🍌 is ⬡ .

🌲 A 🍃 is ⬡ .

Alphabet Workbook

 Read the sight words and then underline the correct picture.

a big

a big

Alphabet Workbook

Mm

 Words that end the same are called **rhyming words**. Look at each picture and say its name. Draw a line to match the rhyming picture.

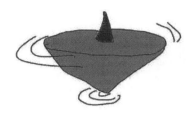

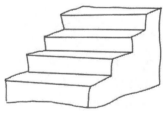

Alphabet Workbook

Look at the picture of the cat. Draw a line from the cat to each picture whose name rhymes with cat.

Alphabet Workbook

Name the first picture in each row. Look at the other pictures in the row. Circle the picture whose name rhymes with the first one.

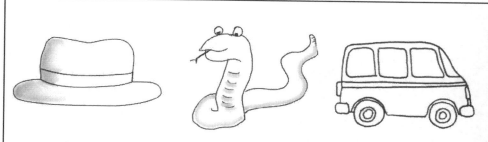

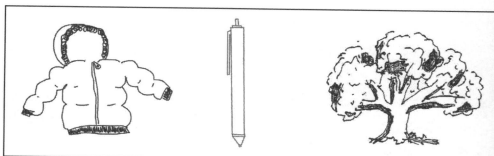

Alphabet Workbook

 Look at the pairs of pictures and the words beneath them.
Circle the pairs that **rhyme**.

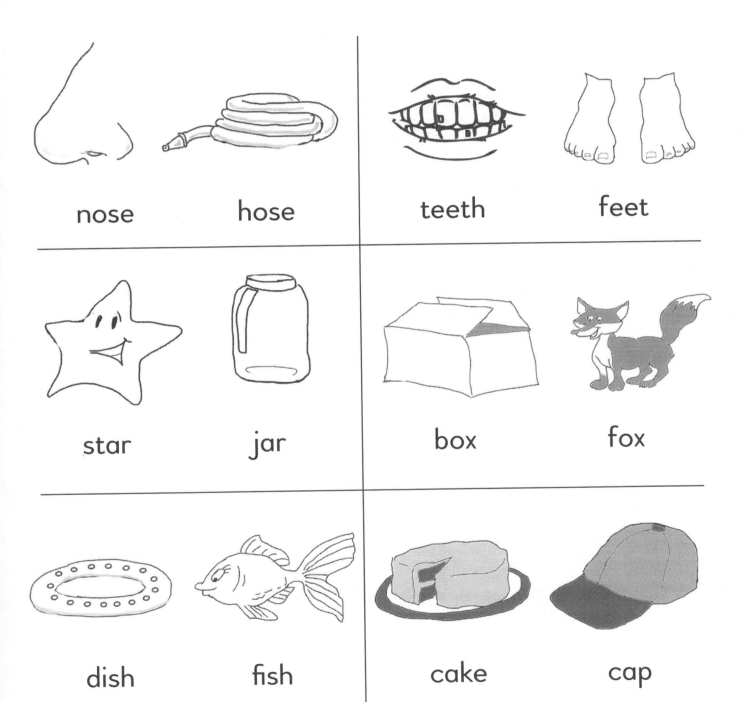

nose	hose	teeth	feet
star	jar	box	fox
dish	fish	cake	cap

Iphabet Workbook

© Heritage Text

Mm

Look at the pairs of pictures and words.
Circle the ***rhyming*** pairs.

map	nest	dog	frog
hat	bat	kite	mop
can	fan	rat	hen

Alphabet Workbook

 Practice the letter **M**.

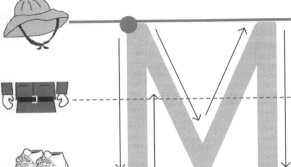

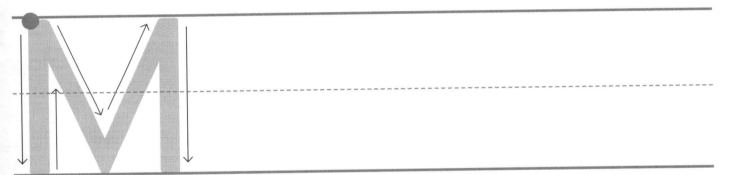

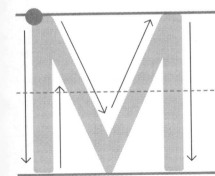

Alphabet Workbook

Practice the letters.

Ma

Mr.

MD

mad

Alphabet Workbook

 Practice the letters.

Ma

Mr

MD

mad

Iphabet Workbook

Mm

 Color the capital **M**s blue. Then color the lowercase **m**s yellow to reveal a hidden picture.

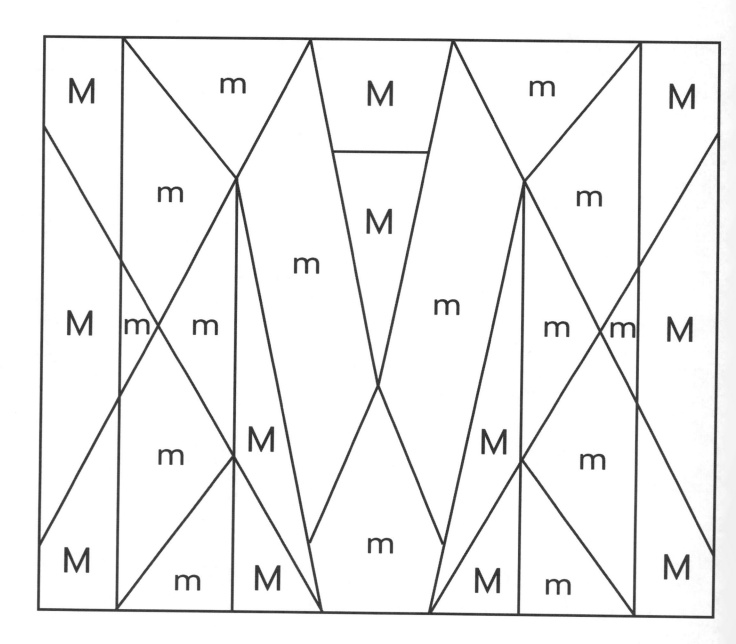

© Heritage Text

Alphabet Workbook

Draw pictures of words that begin with letter *p*

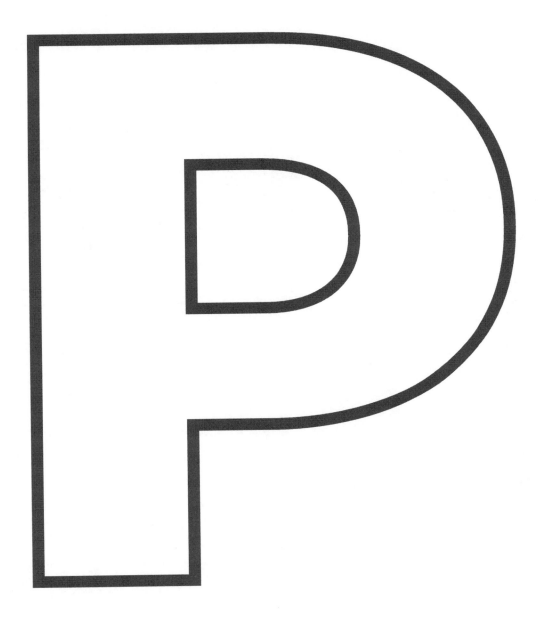

Write the letter **p**.

Alphabet Workbo

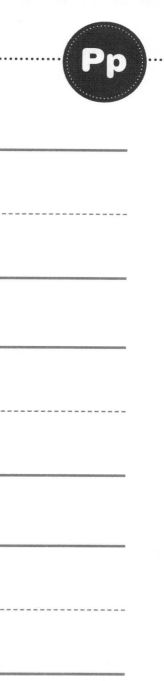

 Write the letters *p*, *m*, *pa*, and *pr*.

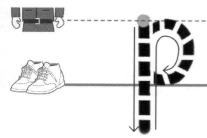

p

m

pa

pr

Iphabet Workbook

Pp

Write the letters **p**, **nap**, **pan** and **map**.

© Heritage Text

Say the name of each picture. If you hear the /**p**/ sound at the beginning draw a line to the *pencil* in the middle.

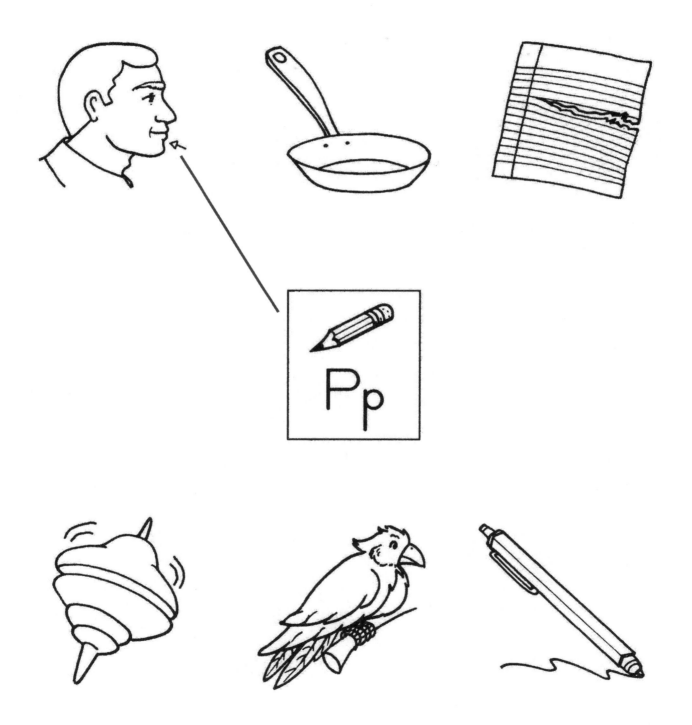

Iphabet Workbook

Pp

 Say the name of each picture. Color the picture whose name has the same ending sound as **map**. Write the the letter **p**.

_ p   Name _____

1.

p

2.

3.

© Heritage Text

Alphabet Workbook

 Say the name of each picture. Write the letter **p** under each picture that has the same ending sound as **map**.

Name _____

p

Alphabet Workbook

© Heritage Text

Listen for Pp

Help the [horse] get to the [fence]. Say the name of each picture. If it begins with the sound for

p, [crayon red] it red. If it ends with the sound

for **p,** [crayon yellow] it yellow.

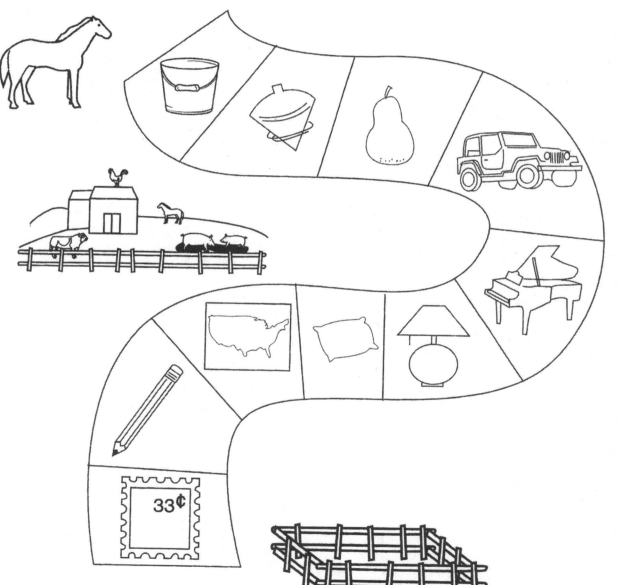

Alphabet Workboo

 Cut out the letters on the left. Paste them into the spaces on the right to make words.

Name

Make Words

N	n	a
r	n	a
D	d	a
m	m	a
p	p	a

Alphabet Workbook

© Heritage Text

 Cut out the *vowel*. Paste it onto a stick. Use the stick to practice blending the vowel before and after each consonant.

Name

a

n

r

d

m

p

Iphabet Workbook

 © Heritage Text

Name each picture. If the picture begins with the sound **p**, draw a circle around the first **p**. If it ends with the sound **p**, draw a circle aroung the second **p**.

1.

p   p

2.

p   p

3.

p   p

4.

p   33¢   p

5.

p   p

6.

p   p

7.

p   p

8.

p   p

9.

p   Liberty 1999   p

 Read the word, tap out the sounds of the word. Then, circle the number of sounds and write the word on the line.

map	1 2 3 4 5	------
ram	1 2 3 4 5	------
dam	1 2 3 4 5	------
dad	1 2 3 4 5	------
pad	1 2 3 4 5	------
mad	1 2 3 4 5	------

Alphabet Workbook

 Name the pictures on the page. If you hear the /**p**/ sound at the beginning turn the line into a **p**, and if you hear a /**d**/ sound at the beginning turn the line into a **d**.

Iphabet Workbook

Read the word. Write it on the line. Circle the correct picture.

p a n

_____

- - - - - - - - - - - - - -

_____

m a p

_____

- - - - - - - - - - - - - -

_____

p a d

_____

- - - - - - - - - - - - - -

_____

n a p

_____

- - - - - - - - - - - - - -

_____

Alphabet Workbook

on

it

Iphabet Workbook

Pp

Read the first word in each row.
Find the same word in the row and circle it.

on	(on) and
it	is it
I	a I
and	that and

© Heritage Text

Alphabet Workbo

 Read the sentence. Draw a line from the sentence to the matching picture.

Name

A man **is on** a pan.

It is Nan.

It is a ram.

It is on a map.

lphabet Workbook

© Heritage Text

Practice reading.

1. pan
2. map
3. man
4. Pam
5. nap

6. rap
7. dam
8. mad
9. ram
10. pap

1. <u>The</u> map.
2. <u>I like the</u> map.
3. <u>I like the</u> map <u>not</u> dad.

1. <u>That</u> ram.
2. <u>That</u> ram <u>and a</u> man.
3. <u>That</u> ram <u>and</u> man rap.

© Heritage Text

Alphabet Workbook

 Name each letter and the sound it makes. Then count the number of **p**'s and **d**'s there are and graph it on the bottom by coloring in the boxes.

p	d	d	p	p	p
d	p	p	d	p	d
p	p	p	d	p	p
d	d	d	p	d	d

p	d
p	**d**

phabet Workbook

Practice the letter **P**.

Alphabet Workbook

 Practice the letter **P**.

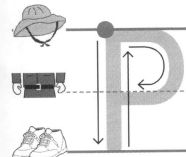

P

Ann

Nan

Pam

Pp

 Color the capital **P**s purple. Then color the lowercase **p**s pink to reveal a hidden picture.

P	P	P	p
P	P	P	P
P	P	P	p
P	p	p	p
P	p	p	p

Alphabet Workbook

Draw pictures of words that begin with letter **s**

Write the letter **s**

© Heritage Text

Alphabet Workbook

 Write the letters **s**, **sa**, **sad** and **pad**.

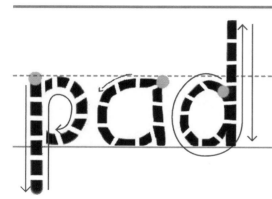

phabet Workbook

 Write the letters **ss, pass, mass** and **sap.**

© Heritage Text

Alphabet Workbook

Trace the letter **Ss**. Say the word that names each picture. Color each picture whose name begins with the same sound as *sock*, and draw a line from these pictures to the letters **Ss**.

Name _____

Alphabet Workbook

© Heritage Text

Ss

Trace the letter **s**. Say the word that names each picture. Color each picture whose name begins with the same sound as *sock*.

Ss Name _____

_____

_____ S _____

_____

_____

_____

_____

7 9

Alphabet Workbook

 Say the name of each picture. Draw a circle around the letter that stands for the sound you hear at the beginning of each picture name.

Name _____

 Say the name of each picture. Circle the letter that you hear at the end of each word.

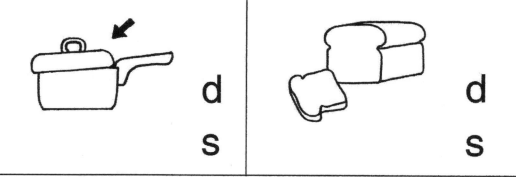

phabet Workbook

© Heritage Text

Ss

 Say the picture name. Write the letters that stand for the beginning and ending sounds in each picture name.

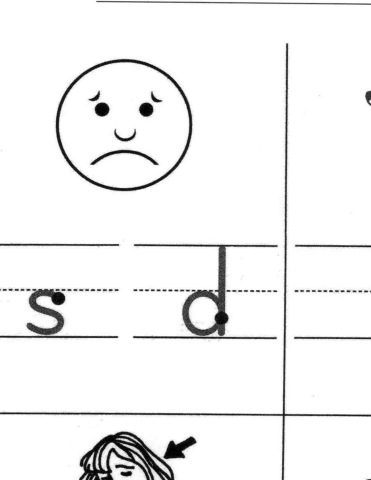

s   d

_____ _____

- - - - - - - - - - -

_____ _____

_____ _____

- - - - - - - - - - -

_____ _____

Alphabet Workbook

In each row, put an **X** on the picture whose name does not begin with the sound **s**.

1.

2.

3.

4.

5.

phabet Workbook

Say the name of each picture. Draw a circle around the letter that stands for the sound you hear at the beginning of each picture name.

Name _____

Alphabet Workbook

Ss

 Read the word, tap out the sounds of the word. Then, circle the number of sounds and write the word on the line.

sad		
sap		
pass		
mass		

 Read the word, then draw a picture.

m a n

s a d

m a d

r a n

Alphabet Workbook

Look at the pictures and the words under them. Draw a line under the word that names the picture and write it on the line.

mad ham

mad

Nan man

_____

an   sad

_____

man mad

_____

© Heritage Text

Read the sentences.
Draw a picture of one of the sentences.

1. Sam ran.

2. Dad ran.

3. A man ran.

4. Dan ran.

5. A ram ran.

6. A sad man ran.

7. A mad man ran.

Alphabet Workbook

Cut out the letters on the left. Paste them into the spaces on the right that are missing letters to make words.

Name

Make Words

s	n	a
u	r	a
p	d	a
m	m	a
p	p	a

phabet Workbook

 Cut out the vowel. Paste it onto a stick. Use the stick to practice blending the vowel before and after each consonant.

Name
_____

a

n
r
d
m
p
s

phabet Workbook

177

© Heritage Text

Alphabet Workbo

said

not

Ss

Read the first word in each row.
Underline the same word in that row.

said	<u>said</u>	sad
not	not	nut
I	a	I
on	in	on

 Read the phrases. Draw a line to match
the phrases to a picture.

| Dan said |

| the man said |

| Sam said |

| Nan said |

phabet Workbook

© Heritage Text

Read the sentences.

It is Nan.

It is <u>not</u> Nan.

It is Dan.

It is <u>not</u> Dan.

Alphabet Workboo

 Read the sentences. Then draw a line under the word said.

Dad said, "Dan!"

Dad said, "Nan!"

I said, "Dad!"

Dad

Dan

I

Color the pictures that are the SAME SIZE.

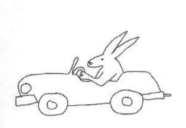  

phabet Workbook

Ss

 Circle the LARGE picture in each row.
Then color the pictures.

Alphabet Workbo

Practice the letter **S**.

phabet Workbook

© Heritage Text

Ss

 Practice the letter **Ss, Sd, Sp, Sam**.

Ss

Sd

Sp

Sam

Alphabet Workbook

Color the capital **S**s purple. Then color the lowercase **s**s pink to reveal a hidden picture.

Color the capital **S**s purple. Then color the lowercase **s**s pink to reveal a hidden picture.

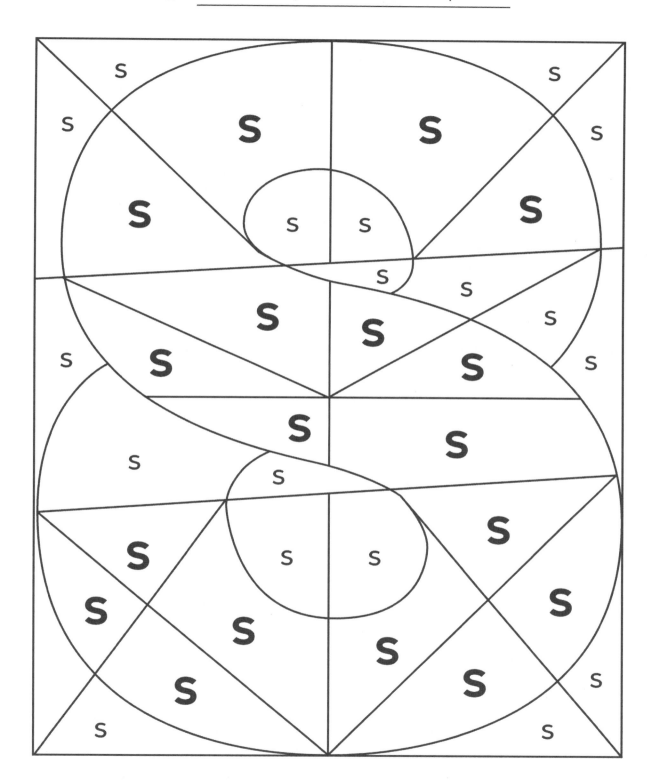

© Heritage Text

 Draw a line to match the capital letters with the correct lowercase.

A	n
D	R
P	a
M	s
N	d
R	m
S	p

Letter S Workbo

Draw a line to match the letter to a picture that begins with that sound.

Aa

Nn

Rr

Dd

Mm

Pp

Ss

tter S Workbook

© Heritage Text

Practice the letters.

a A

n N

r R

d D

Letter S Workbo

 Practice the letters. Then write your name.

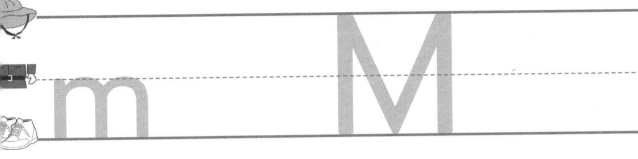

m　M

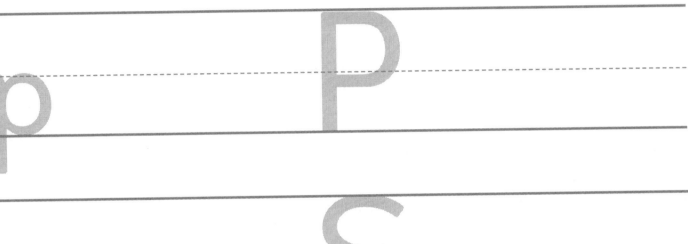

p　P

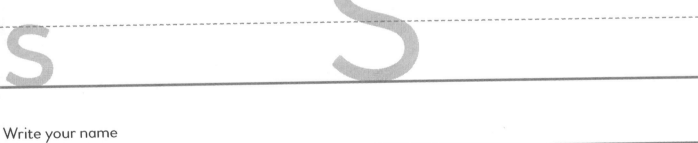

s　S

Write your name

Letter S Workbook

Made in the USA
Middletown, DE
13 September 2024